Colors of The Soul

Colors of The Soul

A Poetic Quest

Merle P. Martin

Gray Dog Press

Colors of The Soul
Copyright © 2009 Merle P. Martin
All Rights Reserved
Printed in United States of America

For information:
Gray Dog Press, 2727 S. Mt. Vernon #4,
Spokane, Washington 99223

www.GrayDogPress.com

Layout, design and editing: Gray Dog Press

Except for brief quotations during review, no part of this publication may be reproduced in any form or by any means, electronic, mechanical, and recording or otherwise without prior written permission of the author or publisher.

ISBN: 978-0-9822743-0-9

Foreword

What is the soul? We have been seeking answers to this question for thousands of years. We have theories, but no evidence. Perhaps this is the way the soul is supposed to be – an entity that each of us must define to fit our individual realms. To me, the soul is not a thing, but a cubicle of being measured in dimensions yet unknown. To me, the quest for the soul is as important as the soul itself.

What are the colors of the soul? Does it have colors, in perceptions of which we currently are allowed? I do not know, but I can envision there being colors. Soul colors, or lack thereof, is a part of my quest – is a part of this collection of poetry.

That quest begins with our inherited and acquired doubts and insecurities. It ends with resolution, not necessarily of what is the soul, but that it exists – wherever, whenever, in whatever form. The journey between encompasses our awareness and acceptance of where and what we are, including that rollercoaster existence that we call love.

Many of these poems were written for my ever-bride, Dotty. All were inspired in some part by her. However, I dedicate this book to the late Dr. Clarence (Clem) Simpson of Terra Haute, Washington. I never met Clem personally, although I was anticipating that meeting eagerly. We communicated occassionally by telephone and e-mail. Nevertheless, our primary exchange was through letters. Dr. Simpson encouraged this man in his 70s to write his first poetry book – and so I did.

He once had been Chairman of the English Department for Whitworth College in Spokane. He had taught at several other institutions as well. Yet, in my mind, his most striking accomplishment was doing so in a wheelchair and on crutches. His youth-diagnosed polio never stopped Clem. He was teaching at age 95 until the time of his death. I am sorry that the poetry that I surely will write for and about Clarence Simpson will not appear in these pages. Yet, appear they will - in subsequent efforts. Thank you, Clem, for your short but magnifiscent visit to my life.

I also thank Tom Sexton, former Poet Laureate of Alaska, for his valuable pre-reading of this manuscript.

Please join us in this quixotic quest for the colors of the soul.

Merle P. Martin, PhD
Spokane Valley, WA 2009

Table of Contents

Footprints — 1
*"He stumbled, he fell
his flesh much too weak
to support his soul."*

Dayspring — 39
*"I need no spectacle to spur me,
other than lunar eclipses,
Pacific swells, a tooth-gapped
child's smile."*

Flames and Embers — 59
*"Before it grasps sunglow reins,
I whisper to the dawn,
Be gently hazy for a while,
until her dreams are gone."*

Moonspring — 87
*"Life's but a gypsy's song
staged by playful god. So,
perform, young puppet, perform!"*

Publication Acknowledgements — 105

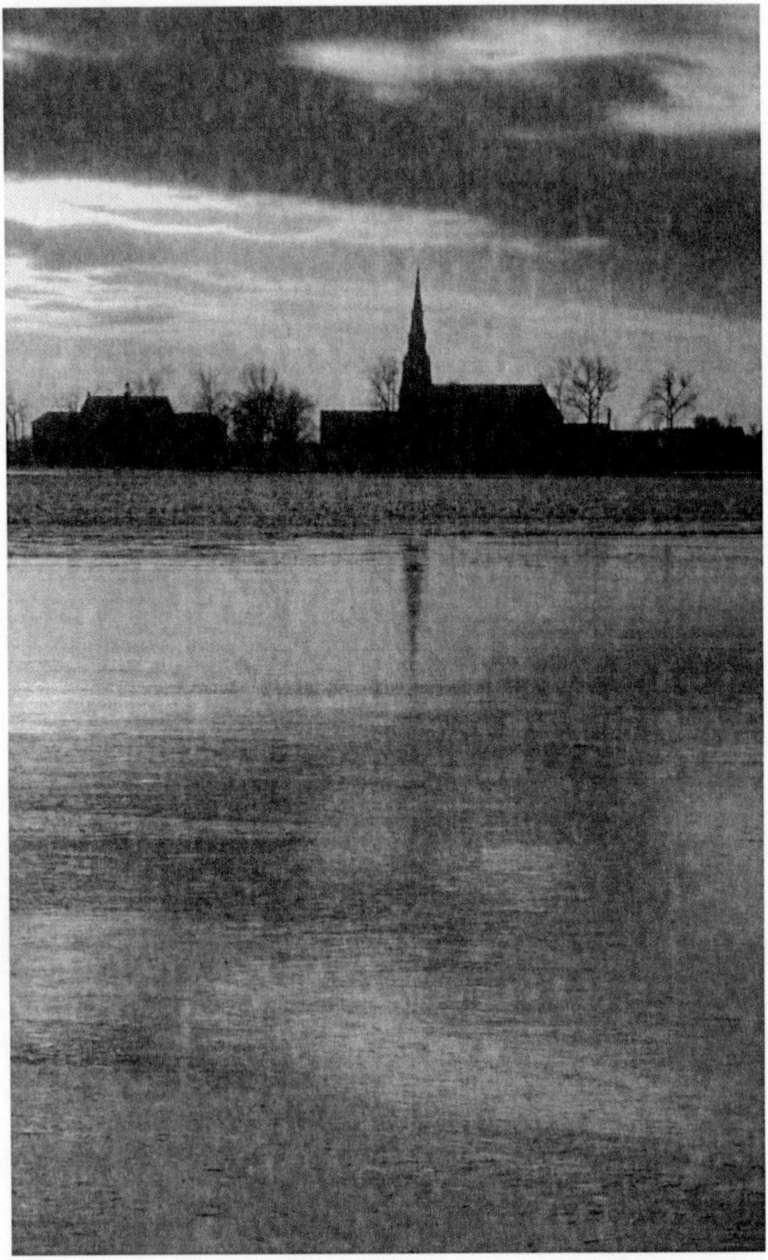

Footprints

Don Juan's Dying 2
Whispers from Antiquity 4
The Young Guru 6
Mirror Ciquain 8
Golden Gate Bridge 8
Symphony of the Absurd 9
Questions 12
Whiskey Joe Revisited 14
Knight of the Sad Countenance 16
The Bench 17
Glow 18
Tides 18
Unshackled 19
Before the 8.4 20
Dorian's Portrait Reframed 22
East of Brigadoon 24
Displaced Heroes 26
Patience 28
The Blackboard 30
Walk in the Shoes 32
Within 34
Conduit 36

Don Juan's Dying

My folly to enmesh
myself in fleshes' lures,
excluding otherwise.

Suns rise to dawn's baton.
Spades will know their gravestones.
I breech women's souls.

My legion of senses
marches to rapture's peaks,
in Bolero crescendo.

Higher, higher.
Faster, faster.
Symbols crash!

Stars explode, volcanoes erupt,
All of me flows from me.
I transcend mortality!

The dance is done!
My cosmos collapses to
chasms of passion's passing.

Fulfillment plunges swiftly,
scant time to prepare for
rhythm-sparse normality.

Afterness numbs,
expectations unfulfilled,
until urges wake.

Lust stumbles out,
searches about
for other heights to climb.

My conquest symphony.
will long live with me
in history strains.

He whispers softly, as he
dies with slightest smile,

My dance is done.

Whispers from Antiquity

Do not dread days ahead.

I speak from sun seasons
mislaid before Pharaoh's tomb.
I built a Sphinx, planned pyramids,
trekked Antarctica's forests.
I am before your before.

Immersed in energy's seas,
I sense tremors of which worlds consist,
bid unseen laws that you could know
if unfettered of left-brain dogma.
Thus, I persuade events about me.

I am Orion of sundry paths,
Quetzalcoatl and Bahaullah,
seeding lost skills and knowledge,
secrets of celestial precession,
in cultural myths and legends.

I have survived star ascensions,
earth and ocean agitations,
Ice Age comings and goings.
Many species have become extinct,
while we stay eon-linked.

Cultures rise, languish, rise again.
Yet, truth remains unchanged,
simpler than you imagine.
Consider that geometric *pi*
is but 22 divided by 7.

So, you need not reinvent.
Merely uncover those messages
long buried in my footprints.
In addition, consult your soul.
You know more than you know.

Do not dread days ahead.
Heed star-tide flowings.
Apocalypse is but fact revealed.
It is then that you will recognize
you are of what has been said.

The Young Guru

The old Irishman chortles,
"Don't be morose, dear lad.
This pub won't serve the sad.
Come listen here.
My grand pappy used to
sing me this drinking ditty:

*Had we a ladder to what will be,
our weary eyes might finally see
that everything's designed,
staged carefully by time,
then botched by us to comedy.*

*Beyond us unfound planets glow
in colors we have yet to know,
but we can't choose at all
how to paint our own walls,
so let's just let creation flow.*

*When eating a rum and whiskey cake,
don't ask if the ingredients are fake.
If that thought causes dread,
pour more booze on instead,
and enjoy the cake, for God's sake.*

So, do not grieve, my lad.
Have another on me.
That's all that's real
for the hither now."

Life as a limerick?
How simple.
How plain.
How easy to explain.

Mirror Cinquain

Wrinkling,
hair shrinking, grey,
with dandruff, paunch, eyelids
sinking. Shaving's become a lot
less fun

Golden Gate Bridge

Morning fog has vanished
replaced by traces of smog.
Sculptured city,
inverted canyon of prim glitters.

That other span fading to
fear-crazed Oakland.
Alcatraz and Angel islands
suck white-tipped waves.
Marins's singed hills.

Last scene for so many who,
immersed within,
wanted to see no more.

Symphony of the Absurd

She steps hesitantly toward the door,
lips life thin, thoughts colliding.

*"I'm not going to commit my dad to
some dismal den. This place had
better be as good as they said."*

Robert rises at five, combs his butch white hair,
fumbles on a dress shirt and black suspenders,
hobbles to the nurse's station for staff brewed coffee,
entertaining Whining Betty, the Frenchman,
and Huge Susan - a jester in kings crown.

Then he moseys down to the dining room
to inspect a just-posted breakfast menu.
He treks all wings shouting out selections
like a medieval town crier,
then rushes to the front door at eight
when the facility opens to visitors.

*"The lobby looks pleasant and this woman
greeting me seems professional enough.
But who's that guy with
butch-cut and black suspenders
waving frantically from the back?
He looks like a Wal-Mart greeter."*

Ragtag procession of wheelchairs
and squeaky walkers twisting ahead
to the dining room where
deliberately overcooked meals wait.
Each resident sits at an appointed table.

An old zombie movie flashes through her mind.
She jumps in surprise.

*"What's that? Oh, it's a blackish
cat rubbing against my ankle."*
What's she doing in here?

Darkened rooms with forms frozen to their beds.
A TV blasts from a room on the left.
Guttural sounds echo from a head hanging
off a wheelchair in a busy aisle.
Soft sobs sift from a room ahead
A slight hint of urine wafts like alien perfume.
A nurse yells at an aide, then
coos lovingly to a waiting wheelchair resident.
Laughter explodes in a distant wing.

The bedlam bewilders her as her guide babbles on.

"What sort of place is this?"

Orientation concluded, she starts to leave,
passes an activity room where
caged birds coo and shriek and a
table is filled with penny-ante poker players:
Robert, Ivan, John, and some sculptured lady
who can barely reach the table top.

The house cat brushes against her leg again
as she passes an empty ice cream parlor,
and a sign announcing a memorial service
for a former resident.

As she reaches the door, Robert bolts from
his poker game, rushes outside to wave goodbye to her.
As the door closes, she hears laughs competing with moans.
She steps around an ambulance as she wanders to her car,
conscience thawing to tears.

"Oh, Dad, Dad, what am I going to do with you?"

Questions

A poem is a question.

Certainty? It lies not there.
Scarier than the idiot
is he who does not know
that he does not know.

Found truth is but a crossroad.
The more we learn, the more we find
there is too much for us to learn.
Education is structured ignorance.

And learning devours time's flesh.
Just when we think we can see
that blurry path before us,
we've lost means to walk it.

Then, why learn at all?

To learn is to live – to live to learn.
One cannot begin fourth grade
without starting out in first.
Who knows where diplomas lie?

Consider the poet.

The poem seeks but never finds;
each word, each stanza reaching.
The poet cannot grasp its meaning,
even if readers are willing to try.

For, a poem is but a question
not begging for an answer.

Yet.

Whiskey Joe Revisited

"Fourth Avenue Whiskey Joe,
stinking away the day
in a cluttered traffic court.
Hand for a pillow, chin attached to chest,
he groans asleep, explodes to snores,
then snaps awake, eyes darting,
as if he'd swallowed yesterday."

I wrote this poem thirty years ago,
not knowing it would haunt me.
"Swallowed yesterday"? Can that be?
With ample whiskey or drugs, maybe.

". . . on a ship dead at anchor in an ice-locked bay."

If we bury what has been,
it grows cactus-like,
shockingly painful to remember,
not blunted by frequent revision.
Regurgitated truth is difficult to swallow.

"The windows crack; they are coated with me."

Tell me, my son Charles,
why did you choose to melt into
San Francisco fifteen years ago?
Paranoid Schizophrenia, they say.
It soothes guilt if repeated enough.

"... *silence the bone-ache of leaving you.*"

Was that you I saw on Market Street,
arguing with your discordant voices?
Do you sleep in crowded courts,
roar snores, snap awake,
as if you'd swallowed yesterday?

"*Perhaps, my friend, I shall mourn you after I am gone.*"

My lost son, I cannot bury our yesterdays,
in hopes they will point to our tomorrows.

Italicized phrases by Charles P. Martin in **Fineline Thunder**,
Devil Mountain Press, 1986

Knight of the Sad Countenance

The cane-propped man stoops still,
clutching a finely carved piece
of that myth who dared windmills.
Nodding his etched head, he speaks.

   "He had this unlikely dream, more so it seems
   because his years had stolen means to achieve.
   One fact divides real life from would-be dreams.
   Age plays at youth in sleep – dawn's the grief
   of traitorous muscles.
                      Hah! Just look at him,
   back arched to a god-starched posture.
   Could one of such ripe age stand so trim
   for more than twenty seconds and not endure
   spasms for days? I almost shriek his pain."

The oldster drops his treasure.
I leap, catch it before it shatters
on the food-stained floor,
place it his trembling fingers.
Wistful eyes still lingering,
he continues as if nothing occurred.

   "He stumbled, he fell, his flesh much too weak
   to support his soul. His shredded armor bled shame.
   Can anyone alter worlds with bones that creak?
   Still, sometimes my mirror suggests his zest,
     freeing, for an instant, my mind from aging's test."

He plops into his aging chair,
body abandoning flair.

The Bench

I have not been in this park before.
Tired from walking, I sit the bench's edge,
away from the elderly man, so as not to startle.

I sidle glances: age-stitched, regret-stained face;
gravity-weary cheeks almost hiding knife-blade lips;
chin challenging nose in thrust, but not in spread;
uneven, shaggy sideburns; eyes of blackish stone.

He sits motionless – dead, but for shifting eyes.
Watching children playing? Trees weaving?
Squirrels begging? Or just inspecting within?
Rested, I think of leaving when, without moving,
without looking at me, he speaks in raspy tone,

"*Wondrous day, isn't it?*" Before I can respond,
he continues, "*I've been coming here each morning
for over forty years, the last five alone.
The children have changed, cars and buildings too,
but much remains the same, at least in my mind.*

*I've thought lately about not coming anymore –
each step now is a mile – but my bench might miss me.*"
He chuckles, causing him to cough, then continues,
"*The air here is so clearing, regardless of season.
Each breath seems a lifetime.*"

He rises stiffly, adjusts his knitted scarf,
snaps straight his fold-up cane,
begins to limp away. I hear him say,
a few steps from the bench,
"*My lifetime seems only a breath.*"

Glow

Why admire my mind
just because you will not see
my soul's secret glow.

Tides

The ocean's benign spirits
borrow your mind for a time,
return inspiring reflections
to stir within your soul.

The ocean is a poet,
acquiring lover's laments,
sorrow's elegies,
returning buoyant verse.

I miss my ocean sages.
I miss transmuting seas.
I miss their poetry.

Unshackled

He reached where his leg had been, grimaced,
smiled up at his thin-lipped wife.

If I could somehow capture that ghost called time,
as it rides roughshod over what we wish to be,
I'd seize his secrets to ensure my rhyme survived
age's rust, then set the scoundrel free.

My words would carry us beyond far stars
where saga, myth and legend emanate.
We'd not allow earthly shackles to bar,
breaching vaporous gates of simmering fates.

She started to cry. He reached
for her hand, shook his head slowly.

See comets formed, moons cooling. Touch
the edges of infinity. We'll be exempt
from others' laws and rules, mortal crutches
left behind, nothing we'd dare not attempt.

Come with me. Come share my drifting dreams.
Come with me, beyond our body's seams.

He wandered to sleep. She bent down
to kiss his cheek, tenderly said,
'I love you', rose and walked
slowly through the door of his VA ward.

Before the 8.4

The startled tourist freezes at the door
of the roaring, teeming Frontier Bar,
one of many Fourth Avenue saloons
that typify 1960's Anchorage.

Someone once said, "No man alive
can try to walk both sides of this street,
have just one drink in every bar,
and not drop drunk before he's done."

Our cheechako gawks in wonder,
not so much at the gold-rush setting,
but at shouting patrons' range of attire,
chaotic collage ignoring source.

Mukluks and parkas, tee shirts and jeans,
tuxedos and evening gowns,
hunting-vests and knee-length skirts,
military boots and trousers.

The tourist joins the mishmash.

The '64 quake struck hard and sudden
on a rarely quiet, Good Friday afternoon.
The Frontier slid down the steep northern slope,
as did most Fourth Avenue taverns.

Their remains dismantled, whisked away
as trash or reused building parts.
Most saloons were never rebuilt.
How do you recycle an era?

Fourth Avenue now is crammed with stores,
a McDonalds, Post Office, Federal Courthouse,
a bar-and-grill here not there.
No plaque exists to honor the pre-quake street.

That rests to past visitors like me
to bridge shifting chasms of time,
let our hearts explore once more
Fourth Avenue 'before the 8.4'.

Dorian's Portrait Reframed

*I stare at you, lying on your shelf,
last remnant from other years.*

Black, ceramic mug, trimmed in gold,
wide mouth flaring to etched base,
white circle holding an orange and black
emblem of a snorting bull with black wings,
lettered, "13th F.I.S"', "None Shall Excel Them."

I was given you as an eager lieutenant,
first assignment a fighter squadron.
Since, twenty-three moves in forty-eight years
packed, unpacked, repositioned. Yet,
you have not a nick or scratch upon you,
while I am scarred and torn by time's pummeling.

When young, I saw "The Picture of Dorian Gray."
Dorian's portrait ages while he does not.
When he kills, the portrait stains blood.
Dorian's evil life shifts to the picture that
becomes grotesque while Dorian remains
young, handsome, and unsullied, until the end.

Black mug, you likely will outlive me.
Will you be my inverse of Dorian's portrait,
retaining my best, while I display
wrinkles and warts of age, rage and dubious acts?
Will you store the finest of my deeds and thoughts
for those to come, until generations multiply,
after-time fades, and people say, "Who was he?"

Will they pack you away, sell you at a yard sale,
eventually to be found as a relic by future denizens?
Will they know that you hold my soul's purest part?
Will you be able to explain what beauty we can confer
while ever fighting that inner, ugly part of us?
Will you tell them I tried, despite my failings?

> *Oh, untarnished black mug*
> *staring back at me.*

East of Brigadoon

Vladivostok, Russian Far East,
carved from South Asia's jungles.
Closed to the world until 1992,
when communism capitulated.
This 1996 setting captivated me.

Its shielded people, who now could see and be seen,
found gritty truth from visitors and Internet, that
theirs was a relatively humble existence,
despite what Moscow had told them.
After initial shock, anger coalesced.
They began constructing a future.

I'd ride a trolley from city end to end
to ingest old before subsumed.
Dingy harbor off the Pacific suckled bay,
cluttered with rusty ships and docks.

The land slants up through an urban bowl of
broken streets and shallow structures.
Drab, stone stores abut alleys teeming
with peasant vendors in wooden kiosks.
Rotting lots with mural-brightened walls.
A banned church lies blocks from Lenin Square.

The bowl's rim changes to deep, steep forests,
prowled by Asian tigers and massive bears
ready to pounce on any errant human
to reclaim a meal from stolen domains.

The rim's vista is mystical. Stoic skies silhouetting
primordial woods poised over a deep half-bowl of
humanity leading to the sea. I especially recall
those days when sea fog seeped up from the bay,
roof-by-roof, street-by-street, until the city vanished again.

> I don't wish to see it again.
> Vladivostok's mythical *then*
> is too deeply etched in my *now*.

Displaced Heroes

He lumbered to my wounded SUV
on the murky, snow-splattered ramp,
truck's flashing lights blinding me.
Squat, at least 250, filthy jeans, bristly,
ponytail under tattered, greasy cap.
He barked sergeant-like orders,
stomping curses when I did wrong,
softened when he saw my cane,
chattered non-stop to the body shop.

*I'm 60, quitting soon after 40 years.
Started towing in Upstate New York,
lost my twang in 13 years here.*

*Spent 46 months in Viet Nam,
dropped behind lines to save pilots,
lost a leg and two fingers there,
five toes last year to Diabetes.*

*Own land up north of Spokane,
left to me by a Nam buddy.
He died without family.*

I'm also a 'Vietnam-era' veteran,
but spent the war in Alaska,
half a world from dying.
Perhaps it was discomfort at
facing a true war vet or
just 'accident shock'
explaining my behavior.

When we reached the shop,
I lurched from his truck,
hobbled into the office,
scribbled repair forms, had
my grandson whisk me home.

I never said 'thanks' to my tow truck rescuer,
never even asked him his name.
Given our country's icy greeting of
Vietnam heroes, he might
have been used to that,
if you ever get used to that.

Patience

Katrina swallows man's creations.
Biloxi's ancient oaks still stand.

It's not Bangkok skyscrapers, strewn here or there, that snatch eyes. It's pygmy structures, some soot-old, others lately layered. Yet, all are vegetation shrines - not plants, but full-grown trees. Even hovels grudge space.

The sky steps graciously, unaware of its eminence.

Over the Chao Phraye River to Northeastern Thailand, the land's travel-ad green, nature planted with people. Open stalls with thatch roofs, stores with upturned corners, bright dragons painted ground to sky. Rough-hewn Buddha shrines, spirit houses set apart, rutted paths twisting somewhere.

Earth is a silent goddess, older than the shouted rest.

Silky streams nurse murky canals, fitted rocks one side, wooden walls the other. Longboats with cone-hat olds harvesting thrashing fish. An iguana startles.
Sketched shacks etched in bougainvillea, takian vines. A yellow-robed monk stands beside a waterside Wok.

Uncluttered moons glint primeval eyes,
awaiting reclamation.

These people are part of the jungle, no thought that they will dominate. Bangkok wilds are replaced with stone. Here nature reigns. Humans humbly comply.

Ashes to ashes, dust to dust,
peacock steel to rust; time whispers.

We live but seasons to trees, nanoseconds to the sea, never to eternity. For that Thailand moment, I was just a speck of life.
I found strange peace in that.

Katrina swallows man's creations;
Biloxi's ancient oaks still stand.

The Blackboard

*Students arrive haphazardly, clothed in
trepidation, this first semester day.*

He enters at precisely eight
young eyes probing gingerly.

"Another old dude with old dude stories?"

Required freshman class,
students crowding early sections
to secure scarce parking spaces.
Nobody is eager to take this class.
He silently sighs, "I wish I were
teaching a graduate course instead."

"You don't really know us."

He turns to the waiting whiteboard,
imagines it to be a blackboard,
once quaintly commanding,
chalk dust spewing an
aura of competence.

"What's a blackboard?"

Surreal slate never expunged,
radiating pungent sessions
by savants scribbling minds,
wisdom enveloping scholars,
imbuing learning's ecstasy.

"When are you going to start?"

Several minutes past the hour,
he turns back to the class,
begins lessons he has preached
before, and before, and before,
his blackboard loathe to erase.

*"Would you give this lecture
if you were young again?"*

Walk in the Shoes

I-90 off-ramp, youngish man panhandles a captive line of cars.
Unshaven, weather-carved face, scraggly hair, tee shirt,
rumpled denim coat. I'd better not meet his eyes.

He's homeless – not the spawn of Jack the Ripper!

Cardboard shelter for his mangy dog – a companion or security.
Battered backpack strewn aside, sign, 'Need Money for Food'

13 percent of homeless have mental health issues.

I'm truly sorry for that. My son has wandered San Francisco for
fifteen years.
When we try to coax him off the street, he disappears, to be alone
with his voices,

22 percent are children, six percent victims of domestic violence or evicted from their homes, nine percent have alcohol or drug addictions.

What are you – a vagrancy digest? Well, that guy's not a child or
woman who's suffered violence. As for eviction, there's plenty of
homeless shelters on the Internet. Alcohol addiction? Hey, I've
been there, but didn't hit the streets.

You could drive him to a shelter or rehabilitation center.

And make me late, let him stink up my car, mug me on the way?
There are people paid to do that. I donate to United Way.

70 percent of them have no income

I've seen 'Help Wanted' signs at several fast food places.
He'd have to shave and shower - at some shelter, I suppose.

You seem a master of rationalization.

How do you spot the 25 percent really down on their luck?
Do they carry certification? Is this just another bum thumbing
across country, mooching change for drugs or booze? Signal's
green. I'm driving now, don't want to think about him anymore.

How do you know that he wasn't one of the four who really needs you?

Shut UP!

Within

If my outer eyes could no longer see,
my inner eyes would fashion ecstasy.

Lying awake in bed at night,
my outer ears hear wind gusts.
My inner ear perceives these
as waves washing pristine shores.

A stranger brushes my arm.
I pull away instinctively.
When my love touches,
my heart courses quickly.

My outer eyes acquire
trees in seasonal decay.
My inner eyes convert these
to queens in noble array.

Our outer senses gather
minute electric pulses,
that our inner senses sift,
send the worthy to our brains.

Some processed pulses progress
to the heart, in time the soul,
wherein lies antiquity's code
to who and why we are.

So, when you feel a satin sleeve,
or smell fresh oven bread,
let inner senses transcend you
to vistas of tranquil knowing.

What we perceive is never real
until our inner self reveals.

Conduit

Can you see that minute star
just beyond the planet Neptune
without a telescope?
Can you hear those hopeless sobs
from starving Darfur children
without latest satellites?

Can you touch antiquity?

Neither can I tell to you
why I write my poetry.
I don't wake up at two a.m.
to invent a hundred reasons.
They'd be but vacuous thoughts,
strained rationalities.

I stare an Autumn tree;
my pen describes an aging princess.
I hear a far train whistle;
it writes of mournful cries.
I clutch my love's soft hand;
my tablet sketches velvet petals.

The truth to my creating verse
is that I never do so.
I am but a rusting conduit,
mirror to a borrowed soul.
For, when it opts to do so,
the poem writes itself,

Can you see what's in your heart?
Can you hear antiquity?

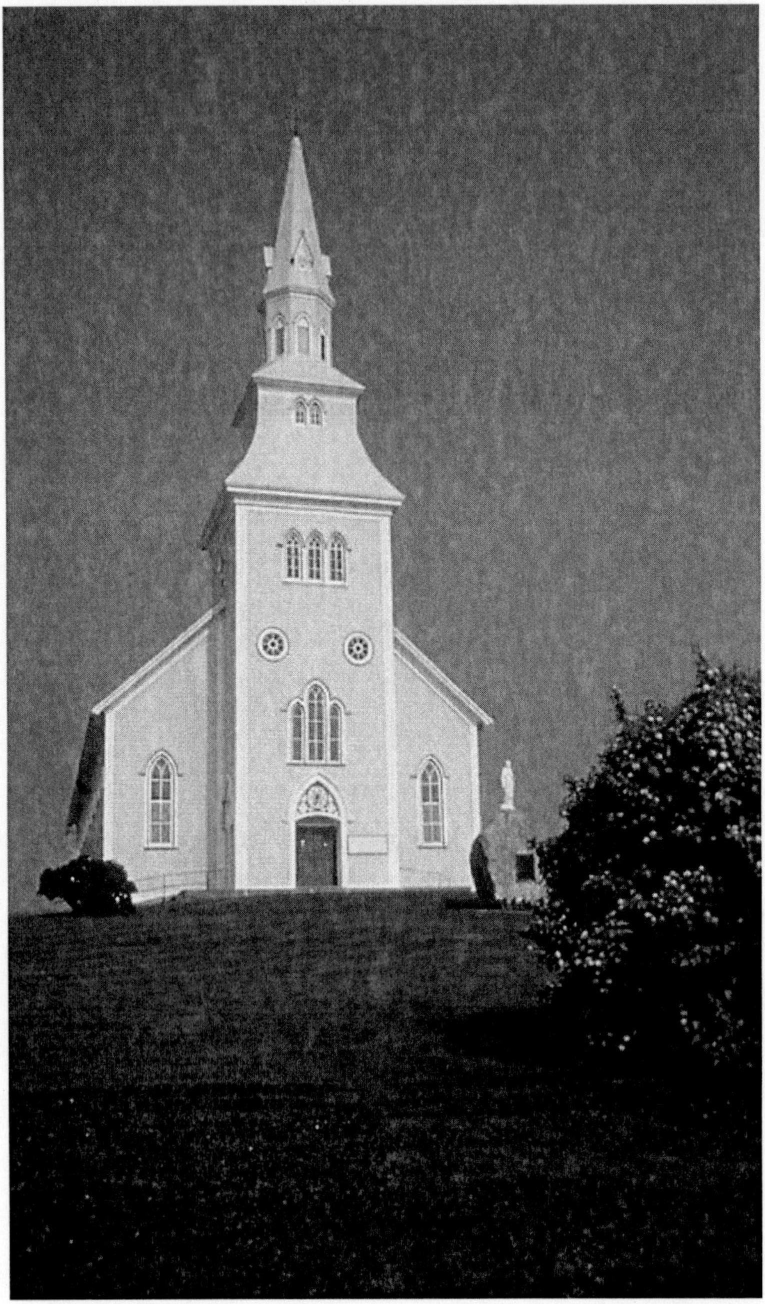

Dayspring

- Time Palette 40
- Silhouettes 42
- Turning 43
- First Fall Morning 44
- Shorelines 46
- Momentary 48
- Return 49
- Late Monday Beach 49
- Seascape 50
- Colors of the Soul 52
- Designs 53
- Glimpse 53
- Inland 54
- Ferry to Bremerton 56
- Seal Rocks 56
- San Francisco 57

Time Palette

Dawn's hint may find me
in mind-sketched galleries.

Lakes mime cobbled shores.
Teeming pines encircle peaks
daubed to ever-whites.
Flocks edge pallid skies.
Hawks hover limb-low.
Gusts lend waters meaning.

Far below, highways hurtle
to stubby, fog-brimmed hills.
Tidy rows of burgeoning trees
nudge knee-high fields
sprouting speckled calves.
Unhurried rivers ripple.

Bridges leap a sun-smudged bay
to sculptured skylines.
Over Twin Peak's rise,
beyond western sprawls,
oceans whisper.

My brush pauses in recall.

Day shrinks.
Lovers drift waves to
nightfall's veil,
silhouettes soon vanished.
Age-jaded sands sift
through wistful fingers.

Bronzed moon:
belying darkness,
dimming stars,
inching skies,
until stroked to
memory's edges,

outside of which
poets pause to paint.

Silhouettes

What seemed an hour was moments.

Snow-laden eaves frame western flames.
Wind chimes whisper vespers.
Naked limbs tremble
as if fearful of twilight's touch.

Moonlight shuns a snow-globe meadow,
deigning only glints of knowing.
Blood red shadows lose hue,
retouching pastel snows to ash.

Utility wires, too thin for distinction,
blend into vanishing branches.
Porch-lights across the road
manifest existence.

The black hole ingests skies,
clouds memories.
Sounds cease.
Earth resolves to darkness.

*I shall sip time's chalice
until acrid night is empty,
and Dawn refills with light.*

Turning

The bus leaves Valdez just after dawn
on its trek by Chugiak northern slopes,
retreating Prince William Sound,
winding north over rocky terrain.

Around an abrupt bend, we see them.
The bus falls still, until the driver says,
"That's the Wrangell-Saint Elias range.
Weather normally ruins this view."

*Three conjoined, ivory peaks
ingesting vast, sapphire skies.
An Autumn-low sun etches southeastern faces,
raising mountains higher than they are.*

*A thin string of clouds acts as bodice,
snowlines as crooked choker.
A minuscule bird edges the stony girth.
This moment begs that it be an eagle.*

The driver shouts departure.
Our reloaded bus begins to move,
silent but for its chugging engine,
unless you think that awe can be heard.

These mountains conspired with time
all other of nature's aspects,
to present a majestic moment,
remind us who we will never be.

First Fall Morning

This temptress day,
this coy Autumn morning,
squishing cemented minds
to seeping awe.

*She whispers,
whispers*

Ivory clouds adorn
chasm turquoise-skies.
Season-leaning leaves
sashay to teasing breezes
that conduct wind chimes
to faint madrigals.

*She whispers
to me*

This temptress day,
this coy Autumn morning,
murmurs tenderly,
"Come to me. Lay with me,
I am Eve in innocence."

*Whispers,
whis-
pers.*

I lash myself to my chair
as Odysseys to his mast
to foil this siren song.

Whispers
to me.

If I go out into this dawn,
this luring Autumn day,
I might mislay the splendor
my poem's eyes now see.

Whis-
pers

Shorelines

Instants drift.

Glistening surges
waltz placid sands,
smear mirror streaks
in stately retreat.

Horizons douse embers.
Twilight bays bleed.

I hover wavering seams
on mislaid wings,
seeking everywhere.

Shadows gather to
dark's soundless beat.

Somewhere it must be rainy,
for there's a distant rainbow.
Varied hues scarcely show,
fulfilled by recollection.

Shrouded surfs persevere,
heedless of time or sight.

My eyes grasp a seashell
lodged in sodden sand.
I dig it out, place it to ear,
as when I was a child on
a seaside much like this.

Dim-lit facades silhouette sands.
Glimmers pass far out to sea.

It whispers to me from
beckoning ocean floors.
I bask in warmth of
lost certitude

Moonlight's bobbing glows
flicker nightened walls.

I wake to practiced guise,
far beaches lapping.

Momentary

A transient bird pauses,
as if the sky had
shelves I cannot see,
plummets earthward
with haunting cries
to the painted pond
across the way from me.

It settles,
dips beneath to
seek its slice of day,
emerges fulfilled,
rises over swaying trees.
With one last linger,
it flies away from me.

Return

Standing alone on a fragile foot-bridge,
crossing the Brazos River.
The wind whips my unzipped jacket,
torments shoreline fronds,
turns water whispers to roars.

I came to scrape away time's rust,
but frantic raindrops batter my uncapped head,
a discarded carton thumps a stanchion,
a jogger enters the slender pathway,
all forbidding me from drifting home.

Late Monday Beach

Sudden seeping clouds, leaking light
puffed enough to muffle sunsets,
spill on paradise.

Hard bodies scurry. Old couples complain.
Fishermen remain,
ageless eyes and patient poles
impervious to change.

Seascape

*Oceans dab away sorrows,
sins from yesterday.*

Gentled waves coax stoic sands,
bequeath foam traces in retreat.
Clouds tiptoe high-flung skies.
Gulls pause, flaunting gravity.
Far islands peek.

Young girls giggle,
fashion sand castles
near oscillating seams.
Young and older lovers sit
hand-in-hand, absorbing dusk.
The molten sun splits to
mirror image spheres,
before wedding languid waters.

Oceans lure as if I loved them.
I fear them.
My idea of swimming is to survive
until help arrives.
Yet, these waters and I
were never strangers.

Scarcely a youthful day passed
when I did not gaze the
Pacific flowing into the Bay;
walk forty blocks to where
lands dare acquiring tides;
wander whispering waves
alone.

Once, I walked here with someone else,
arm in nervous arm.
On these shoreline stretches,
I kissed a girl for the first time.

Perhaps that's why these waters still entice

Colors of the Soul

I am a faith-chameleon,
at ease with believing,
whether it be church or temple,
mosque or synagogue.

Or praying rooftops at sunrise,
silhouette trees at dusk,
mountain streams in spring,
last Autumn fallings.

I am a faith-chameleon,
whether reading Rumi Tuesday,
watching the Science channel Friday,
absorbing a Mahler symphony.

I need no spectacle to spur me,
other than lunar eclipses,
Pacific swells,
a tooth-gapped child's grin.

I am faith-friendly,
inside with others, or
conversing with echoes
in canyons of my soul.

My belief may seem distinctive,
exploring an uncommon path.
Yet, my penchant is collective.
All birds have beaks.

I am a faith-chameleon.

Designs

That stately tree lay naked,
purplish leaves withered away,
until December dressed her in ermine.

Impish winds will try to expose,
but Winter will mend her regal whites,
until Spring can fashion an emerald robe.

Glimpse

The bridge's silhouette
accents seeping nightfall.
Trees are motionless,
in seeming awe of
soundless splendor.

Far mountains ghost.
Waters whisper,
so as not to disturb
dusk's sudden hush,
when time stops breathing.

City lights halo time's portrait.

This is one majestic moment
among many I've enjoyed.
Still, I bask in gratitude
for adding to my memory
one more glimpse of meaning.

Inland

Gas tank to Canada,
stone's throw to Idaho,
I-90 traces the racing river
to Spokane's stumpy skyline.

Harleys, trucks, SUVs,
boat-shops next to hay bales,
Hummer lot near grazing horses,
steeples jutting everywhere.

Otis Grill, 60's style.
Patrons proudly thrusting stomachs,
hefting burly mugs of coffee
with swollen, toil-gnarled fingers.

Unshaven men in NASCAR caps,
woman tee shirts, sequined jeans.
Strip clubs next to grocery stores.
Ballooned car lots every other block.

Mountains erupting evergreens,
puffiest clouds ever seen,
more lakes than you can count,
four non-flaunting seasons.

Faith-stomping, flag-flapping country.
Coastline liberals need not apply.
If you don't like us, don't try to change us.
Go back to where you came from.

Young ones leaving when they can,
to 'anywhere but here',
for 'something to do',
scamper back when they discover:

big cities have tiny hearts,
centerfold hotties have warts,
they need two locks on every door,
they're not seventeen any more.

Ferry to Bremerton

Tiered decks of soft-draped light,
lending her stately whites
ghostly glows that
jewel Puget Sound.
Gliding her wake-less way,
in graceful promenade,
edging to where her path is done,
some place called Bremerton.

Seal Rocks

On that sandy patch
guarding devoured cliffs,
I'd quiver with unremitting tides,
my entire existence abducted below
for a few uncommon moments.

San Francisco

I climbed to almost where the skittish wind
had still to sweep the early morning fog,
wondered how the teeming bay had been
before the buildings' glitter and vessels' clog.

Then stared upon imagined endless seas
as if it were ten thousand years ago,
erasing charted lands from memory,
to sail as then to ends I did not know.

I later strode upon near empty sands,
dreamed I was the first to walk those waves.
When I looked back to where my path began,
my arrogant steps had all been washed away.

I wonder which conceit deceives us more:
how things may be, or what has gone before.

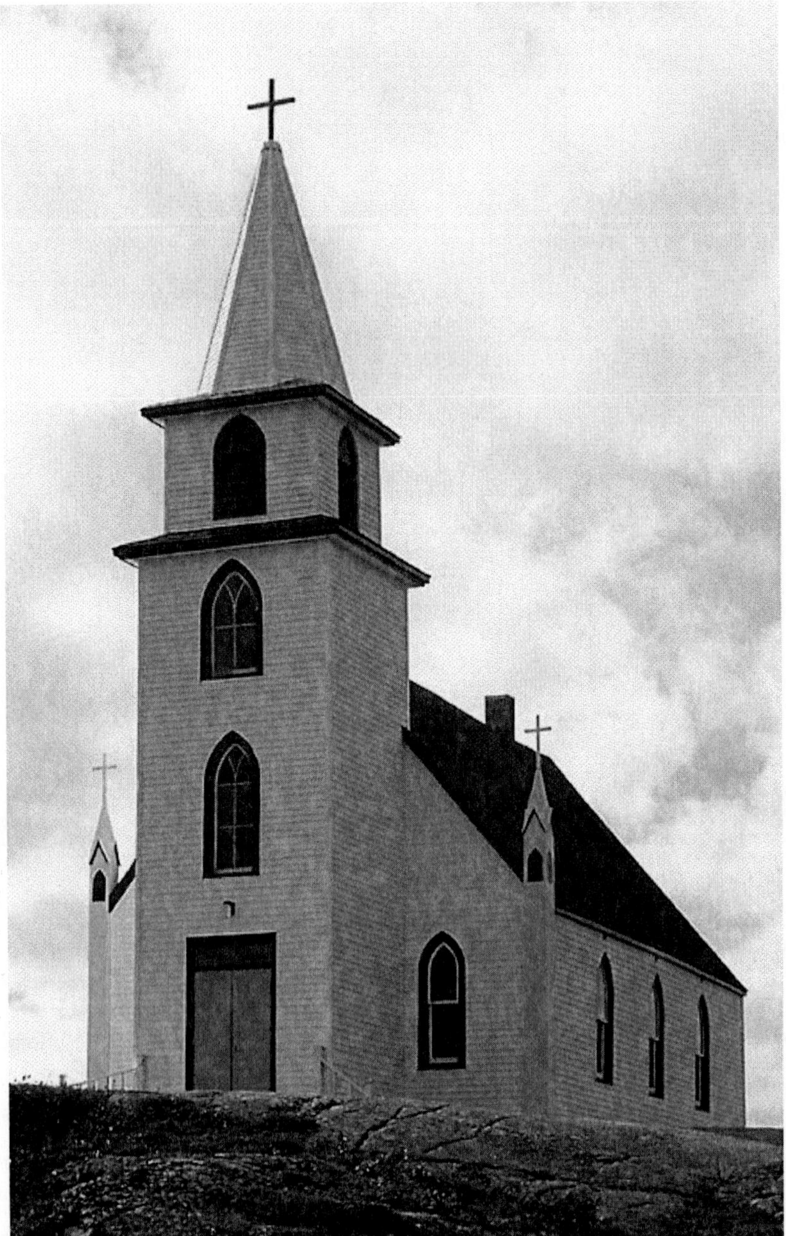

Flames and Embers

Painting Rapture 60
Monterey Revisited 62
Moonlight Musings 63
Wind Quell 63
Slow Rivers 64
Parallel Universe 65
Letter to Afghanistan 66
Time Treasures 67
Never 67
Stealing Moments 68
Meaning 68
Love Legend 71
Nevertheless 72
Time's Mirror 72
First Thoughts 73
Translation 73
Far Song 74
Biloxi 76
Value 76
Time and Roses 77
Awe 78
Sculptor 79
Love Ditty 79
Intensity 80
Cathedral 81
Patricia 82

Painting Rapture

Some say I am a painter of words,
brushing scenes and themes
on whimsy's canvas.

Could I paint morning,
when chants of ancients
swirl above bare awareness,
skies tremble to new-hued light,
and early wings slice horizons
to probing echoes?
Could I paint morning?
I think I could.

Could I paint spring
where snow-soaked peaks
suckle burbling streams,
trees flaunt quivering leaves,
and sudden showers purify?
Where musky breezes tease
and roses remember?
Could I paint spring?
I think I could.

Yet, my thoughts ever
return to your eyes.
How might I capture perfection?

Could a dewdrop sketch a rainbow,
or a gnat a butterfly?
Could a snowflake stroke the cosmos?
Could a leaf depict looming moons,
or a pebble sunset shadows?
How then could I portray your eyes
in words so earthly tethered?

Would that I could borrow Heaven.

Monterey Revisited

Shadows merge.
The bending tree
becomes a silhouette.
Night-triggered lights
begin to build facades.

Below,
surfs still crash,
oblivious to time or sight.
Moments echo.
I bend to listen.
Memories ripple.

We greedily gulped
all that we would have
until it was empty,
and we were still
thirsty

Wind Quell

Our window's trees seem mortified,
now stripped of rust-gold gowns,
their leaves scattered haphazardly
over full-frosted lawns.

Still, by this time tomorrow,
our eyes will be refocused
to find now woeful limbs
in different majesty.

Moments are gems in treasure chests.
When one is removed,
love much more the rest.

So it has been with us.

Moonlight Musings

Another year hugs its precipice
over sodden shoals of memory.
I shall covet always
tomorrow's soaring winds with you,
rather than flail precarious waves of
yesterdays without.

Slow Rivers

Slow rivers wind.

He'd inch the weed-sketched path along
water lappings, stop at the top of the bridge,
douse thoughts in soothing swirls,
try to cleanse ifs and thens.

He always thought that he'd return.

He tried sometimes in night's hidings,
when yearnings flee day's cage,
bygone moons persist,
distant winds whisper;
when remorse thickens
as ice on winter rushes.

He tried sometimes.

Now, in this midnight of regrets,
wistful gusts tapping windows,
he clutches a dislodged leaf,
presses it to recollection,
lest time sweep her
completely away

Slow rivers ever wind.

Parallel Universe

When you try to imagine
a past that never was,
it seems too real for fantasy,
existing in otherness,
a varied version of
this etched waking.

Einstein surmised that
when we choose one path,
forsaking another,
we create an alternate reality
in a yet unknown dimension,
one that's selected our rejected path,
one of an infinite number
of parallel universes.
Poets seem to sense them.

I've visited alternative lives,
those ways untaken.
My mind's discarded every one,
returned home to you.

Letter to Afghanistan

She glances outside,
wipes tear traces away,
begins to write to him.

"Remember when
we would sit sunrise,
hands and souls clenched.

Placid breezes drifting dawn,
nudging night-cloaked leaves
to singing whispers,
melding our morning minds.

Now I watch from inside.
Trees undulate,
as your chest in deep sleep.
The house denies outer sound.
Yet, I still hear leaves humming.

So it is with you.

Even when you are gone
and empty rooms echo,
I feel your vibrant voice
course throughout my being.

I need not hear your laugh.
It cartwheels halls,
caroms off these walls.
It is my symphony of day.

I need not hear your sigh.
It is moon-glow flowing
through undraped windows.
It is my pillow.

I need not hear your voice,
yet cannot wait until I do.
So we can sit mornings,
listening whispers."

Stealing Moments

In first moments of unformed day
when my mind can still soar free
unchained from necessity,
I think of you.

In last breaths of wakefulness
when I try to sketch dreams
for sleep's erratic journeys,
I think of you.

I saw the first spring rose today,
vivid, fresh but strong,
surviving colder times.
It made me think of you.

Time Treasures

As my years too swiftly flow,
and my zest for conquest slows,
I cannot complain.
My treasure remains,
for your love for me still grows.

Never

Never missing
are our days of gentle joy,
never lost
our nights of softed splendor,
never forgotten
our cubicle of rainbow years.

We glean and savor
the most succulent fruit
from allotted orchards.
Never shall we not.

Meaning

If I could touch a rainbow,
breathe the farthest star,
then I might know.
If I could sing a butterfly,
dance a mountain sunrise,
then I might know.

If I could ride the sun
to view creation's art,
or listen to eternity,
I might finally know
true meaning.

Then you enter the room,
and I know that I know.

Love Legend

I dared soar to touch passion's flames.
Charred, I plunged to tortured seas.

Strauss wafts across the lake,
stirring still airs about me.
I stare fluttering flames,
evoking yesterdays.

Drifting from sirens' beguiling,
I washed upon cradling shores.

I've muddled memories,
senses invested in now.
Little focus remains for
discordant passages
once so harshly played.

The princess stood on naked sands.
Lust bowed to pure love's dignity.

Ecstasy's strains enthrall me,
shunning fury that used to be.
Today is excited grace,
songs soft but ever singing.

We ignited our common fire,
stoking coveted flames.

She arrives to sit with me,
to share inner melodies,
beside ardent embers,
ever there – yet,
never consuming.

Nevertheless

It may be snowing,
winds blasting, days dim, but our
love is ever spring.

Time's Mirror

I imbibe your image in morning mirrors,
you brushing hair, still age untainted,
with seamless motions,
jeweled eyes inspecting heaven,
serene yet wistful smile,
carriage hinting ballet lineage.

My imagination floats to when we coalesced as one.
You are still that emerald princess who kissed
this everyday frog, changing me to this blissful now.

How privileged can one man be
to gaze each day a mirror such as this?

First Thoughts

Sounds of muted beauty, hidden yet alive -
motionless, but soaring.
A mere moment stretched beyond,
etching essence.

She owns these moments,
as if they were toys to her touch,
ears to her laughter.

I lie in awe recalling
Dotty in the morning.

Translation

The tiny Chinese seamstress
shyly smiled up to me,
as if we shared a secret
in some cosmic language
that we could only breathe.

Far Song

Khabarovsk, on the Amer River.
Heat and humidity sprint to hell.
Phone in the hall speaks Russian only.
I can't call home to hear her voice,
opt instead to trudge off tension.

Wrinkled Babushka in a wood kiosk.
I point to sausage and bread that she
thrusts at me with dismissive grunt,
snatches coins as if I were a leper.
Block after block, stall after stall,
different wares, same haughty glares.
Marooned on an alien island.

Slumping back, when skies
yield to a hasty storm.
I sprint remaining blocks,
plunge to a darkened room,
strip soggy clothes,
sprawl on the unmade bed,
absorb cool window squalls.

Thunder and lightning rotate.
A stereo echoes through
soaked courtyards below:
Celine Dionne singing.
Closing my eyes, I
imagine that voice to be
she of my ever dreams.

*"Near, far, wherever you are,
I believe that the heart does go on.
Once more, you open the door,
and you're here in my heart, and
my heart will go on and on."*

Alone in a strange, crusty city,
listening in darkness to a song
whose words I can understand.
Sing, my faraway love.
Be with me tonight.

*"And you're here in my heart, and
my heart will go on and on."*

Biloxi

Waters were smoother then,
lulled to warms by
southern connotations.
We'd dare late beaches
along their wavering seams,
then sit edges of that
wind carved pier.
Secret.

I recall your soul-soft eyes.

Depthless,
unedged blues,
reflecting moonlight to
bobbing glows that,
flicker nightened walls,
lap on morning minds.
Even now

Value

If my hands could hold stars,
eyes encompass time's expanse;
if all fact and lore ever known
were lodged within my mind;
their sum would dwarf in worth
your fingerprints upon my soul.

Time and Roses

Whenever I look at you,
it's not with time's shallow eyes,
but angels' borrowed sight.

The rose that bursts to grandeur
withers beyond its season,
but its scent and hue,
it's perfect form,
dwell minds forever.

Our lives have sprouted
rose-like moments
embedded in fallow days.
We wish to be remembered,
not as gust-blown petals, but
for those few exquisite instants
when we conquered time.

I do not welcome years' decay,
but to age with you
is to age with grace.

Awe

Mist-seeping streams.
Foothills etching.
Hovering hawks.
Night sifting away.

Sierra Nevada dawning.

Snow-crests looming.
Waterfall murmurs.
Sudden showers.
Aspen quivers.

Estes Park afternoon.

Montmartre glimmers.
Chiseled alleys.
Silhouette spans.
Cathedral glows.

Twilight on the Seine.

Ember shadows.
Moon-sketched quays.
Pier lights igniting
the shimmering bay.

Monterey at night.

Wonders, all.
Still, my awe
is you.

Sculpture

True meaning waits
deep within its wood or stone
for an artist to sculpt away the
unresolved, freeing it to beauty.

You were that artist -
I, the uncut stone.

Love Ditty

Dawn's light brings me hope.
Even raindrops offer promise,
that I can one more turning cope
with ruts along my trudge to bliss.

For I have you, and that is why
I'll reach Heaven long before I die.

Intensity

The sun's brilliance
sometimes is dimmed by clouds
that form no intentional pattern.
My love is as that sun.

Distractions at time
obscure my love's intensity.
These diversions too
have no purposeful path.
When they are swept away,
my love shines through.
It's been there all the while.

You are my moon, stars gathering about you.
You are my morning, coaxing hope and joy.
You are summer of ease and winter of grace,
rivers winding through my parched heart.

I know that I love you,
for my soul plunges to hell
each time I steal your happiness.

Cathedral

Prelude to primordial day,
nethertime tapping dawn.
Maternal night lingers until
thin strips of shimmering amber
halo far-stretched hills,
ignite etched limbs to dim-lit candles

Sculptured arch of dark-draped clouds
moving slowly yet standing still.
The wall clock measures solemnly
eternity's invocations,
echoing yet hushed.
Life congeals,
mundane matters kneel in
awe.

She enters as the daystar bursts,
shrining her - altar through stained glass.
Specks of spinning gold enfold as she
floats in placid grace to
consecrate my day.

Time weary yet unwavering,
spirit enthralling me
for more than twenty years.
I sense my worth in her eyes,
imbibe hope from her smile,
discern moments of God
reflected in her presence.

My heart now soars
beyond my eyes,

her miracle to me.

Patricia

*Then linger but a moment more,
so I may set your eyes upon the darkness.*

ACT ONE: *Moonfall*

Blue softened eyes
capture a slender face
finely lined with gold
stretched over
shallow shoulders.
Her thin folded fingers
press carefully to her knees
her doll skirt hem.

— — — — —

She laughs at everything,
not laughs, but sings lilts.
Glowing eyes rush waterfall hair.
Her excited hands explode.

(Sing to me,
teach me your delight
so I may hum the slightest tunes.
Sing, my magic one,
I've not smiled hopes before.)

— — — —

In the hush of an ancient evening
we linger
watching the fire age.
Its dwindling glows
shadow walls.
The room bobs softly.

Our asking eyes
then probing lips
seek promises that last,
a pliable future
that's not but a shadow
of the past

ACT TWO: *Darkening*

pale gold hair
framed loosely about
a white canvas face
holding only eyes
grayed to fear

A plastic tube slithers into her face hissing.
Another pumps bloody semen through
violated veins.
A shiny vomit pan awaits its tithe.
Cluttered mourners cast visitations.

(But speak to me, my bedpan lady.
Consult your ventriloquist.
Why do you lie like that?
Why am I watching?
God wears no makeup, but
neither is she naked.)

Five-fifteen,
Front door opens.
Footsteps grope the kitchen.
I leap upstairs to say hello.
She scribbles eyes,
sketches smiles,
fidgets with her wig.

A faded portrait still being retouched,
remembering colors.
(Please whisper to me, my hidden one.
I've glimpsed you in sudden eyes,
heard your laugh echo,
felt you brush my dreams.
I know you're near.)

ACT THREE: *Daystar*

Morning trembles over somber mountains
casting promises to deserted beaches.
Yesterday's darkness slides to muted seas,
while on draining sands, diamonds stir.

A forgotten breeze mingles scents.
A blade of grass tingles to new greens.
The waking pond wrinkles rushing traces.
A rosebush bursts to awareness.

Patricia!
Patricia, your name floats my tongue
as Dawn's gull on cloud-sown skies, soaring,
gliding, pausing in awe of its beauty.

Patricia,
my first breath,
my bridge to god,
come smile with me.
Let's stretch morning moments.

ACT FOUR: Nightless Moons

    rest my weary
    unplug the strobes
    unbuckle your leaden legs
    clutch me
    make my warmth your blanket
    let's hibernate in this
    cubicle of moments

    widowed world
    listen to her skies stiffen
    search her glistening shadows
    stroke echoes of her youth
    cry her roses

*then linger but a moment more
so I may set your eyes upon the darkness*

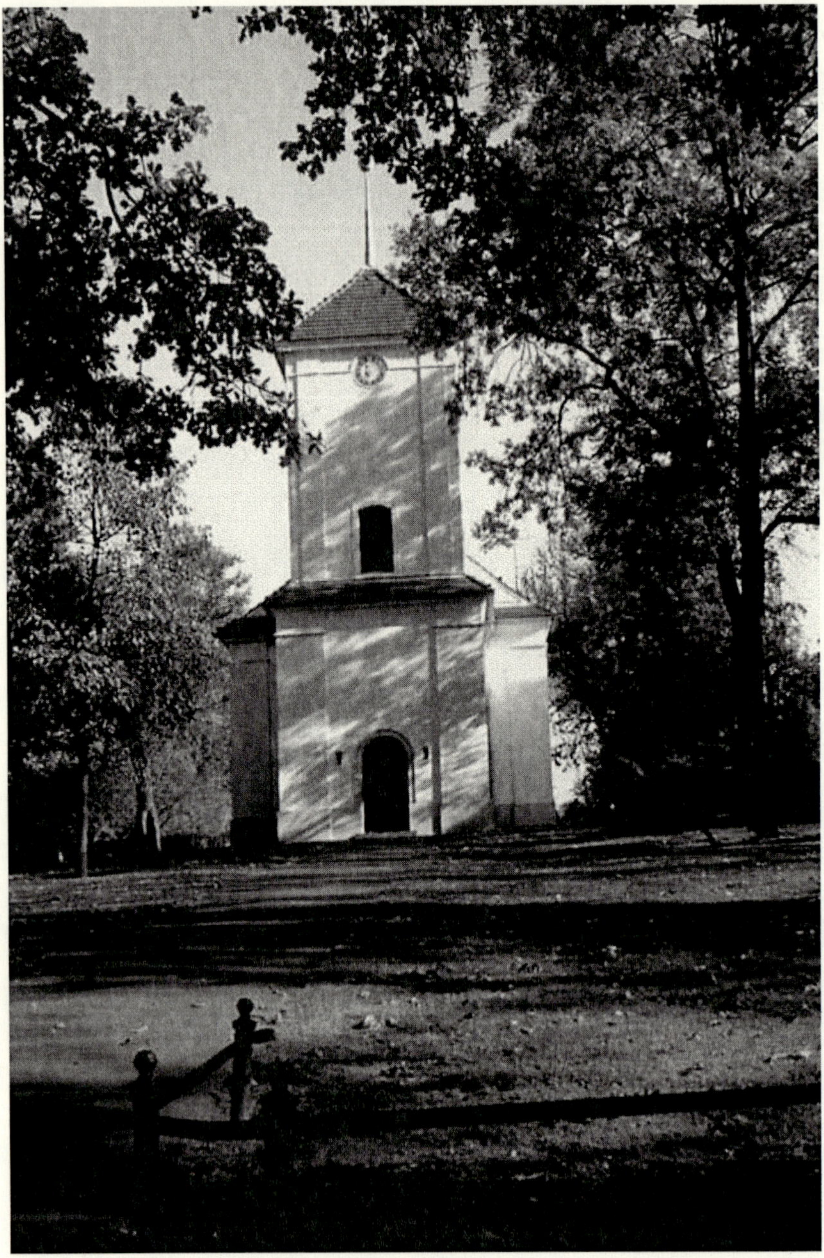

Moonspring

Evolution 88
Hope 88
A Season of Reason 89
Honor 90
Light of Night 92
Tapestry 94
Refuge 94
Morning Suite 95
Paths 96
Personal Destiny 97
Paean to Being 98
Hymn to Further Days 100
Morning Glory 102
Simplest Truth 102

Evolution

I tossed a pebble into the mirror pond.
Responding rings began to grow
there from where it vanished.
In time they touched far shores,
with no recall of that which cast their paths.

Hope

I would be in that day when
love, faith and knowledge
have been knitted into a
bright shawl of certitude.

A Season of Reason

After many months sailing through often turbulent seas,
the Emperor's hundred-oared vessel, peace-ensign
flying high, approached the fortified harbor. There had been
rancorous years embittering these great kingdoms.
The Emperor braved this journey, hoping to soothe this enmity.

But this was not to be.

From the fortresses' thick, impregnable base,
balls of death roared from forty cannons,
falling just short of the anchored vessel.
Seamen began to respond in kind,
when the Emperor signaled to cease.

"We will not amplify strife today, but will
hastily sail away, to return another time
when reason is more in season."
His crew obeyed in stoic fidelity.

Yet some thought this to be cowardice,
that they should have fought as heroes.
One aged sailor shook his head,
"That is why he rules, not we.
He knows best how days to come may be."

Honor

I would honor the artist
striving to catch a shifting sea
over he who paints a fruit bowl
because it's slave to immobility.

I would honor the performer
who fails repeatedly,
rather than the smirking judge
who rarely tries at all.

The former stretches humanity
to where it well might be.
The latter slides us back
to primordial trees.

I would honor the dreamer
who seeks uncertain vistas
instead of she who fails to see
the time-changing forest
for the ritualistic tree.

I would honor the doubter
unsure of many things
rather than another who,
certain of certainty,
knows not what he knows not.

I would honor the scholar
who frees written words
to soar, to twirl, to whirl,
not he imprisoning language
in cages of moldy history.

I would honor the deist or agnostic
who sees in the most miserable
seeds of the majestic,
instead of the zealot
whose majesty is chiseled belief.

I would honor that one who
prefers not to be honored.

Light of Night
(Yancy Revisited)

When dark, I see stars;
when light, meadow trees.
I would not barter one for the other.
Dark yields to light, light to night,
dusk and dawn ease betweens.

Divorced, then my second wife dies,
within a moment of four years.
I plunged from glee to grief's chasm.
Stress attacks, alcohol, and lethargy.

Yet, I had to focus to deter insanity.
I contemplated dusty poetry:
classes, workshops, readings.
Writing has been my companion since.

I was free to move wherever,
to do whatever I wanted to do.
A poster: "Doctoral Candidates Desired."
I applied, was accepted, finished,
found teaching to be my passion.

Yet, before I left, I met Dotty,
not occurring had I been married.
We left Alaska for different places,
reunited and wed four years later.

Late-day love lightens time.
As Yancy said,

*"Life's shadows define bright.
There can be no dark without light.
Living's neither black nor white,
but blending of the two."*

Had Fate not blindfolded my 'then',
I would not be writing this verse,
nor found career-passion,
nor basked in greater love,
nor gazed 'now's' brightness.

When dark, I see stars;
when light, meadow trees.
I would not barter one for the other.

Tapestry

Life's a collage woven on
shrinking fabrics of time,
intricate blending of
hundreds of clashing moods,
threads of disparate hues,
a clever tapestry
hiding me.

Refuge

Yes, these are stormiest times,
but I assure you
there is no urgency of moments.

Share my umbrella of hope.
Follow my path of certainty.
Await rainbows with me.

You need not worry who I am
or where I emanate.
I am no stranger.

I am your tomorrows.

Morning Suite

I wake to light's hums,
hope's morning melody,
when dreams and eyes still
harmonize;
before events score hours
to a hardened symphony.

"The day has a thousand chords."

"Carpe diem," noble Caesar proclaims,
armor rhythmically rattling, "What I think to do
selects the tone for ensuing notes to unfold.
I compose my fate, then chant it valiantly."

"He knows God's song who has sung his own."

"Rubbish!" the old Romanian replies,
through lipless mouth that once knew teeth.
"Life's but a gypsy's song staged by playful gods,
recited by us in words already known.
So, perform, young puppet, perform!"

"My voice echoes in creation's canyons."

Pulses begin. Do I play day
or does day play me?

Paths

Wending my way to somewhere,
leaving neon steeples behind,
brushing regret's limbs aside,
alone but for eons' shadows,
obscuring ancient footfalls.

I peer between thinning skies,
seeking that celestial clock,
cogs, gears and pinions
ticking eternity.
Some bestow on this a name.

On hills beyond blurred lowlands,
I think I glimpse another
of other garb and gait,
seeking his somewhere.
Does he see me?

What if our ways should meet
at the same destination,
and we greet each other avidly
as once-lost, yearned-for souls,
opposites the same?

Are there yet other paths
I've been too blind to see?

Personal Destiny
(On reading Coelho)

Once upon the time, a young shepherd had a recurring dream of a buried treasure. He believed it was his Personal Destiny to discover that trove. He sold his sheep, journeyed to an alien land where other languages and customs prevailed.

He trekked desert sands, seeking omens that might lead to his quest. Along his path, he encountered deceit and kindness, mistrust and welcome, fear of death and promise of ecstasy. After years in search, he discovered an astounding truth. The riches sought were within him. They consisted not of gold nor precious stone, but an infinite supply of goodness and positive energy.

The young shepherd's Personal Destiny was not to find treasure, for that had been within him from conception. His Personal Destiny was to unchain his force so this world could use it to advance humanity, to meld it to its ancient unity, to waft upon all winds this eternal message:

"Man is inherently good. Strive for betterment with patience of angels."

The young man did so, once upon a time – once upon many times.

Adapted from ***The Alchemist***, Pavlo Coelho,
Harper Flamingo, 1993

Paean to Being

Dawn reminds.
I hear a gull's far cry
slicing pristine skies,
"I'm here! I'm here!"
An infant rose unfolding gold
through maternal sheaf repeats,
"I'm here! I'm here!"

My sentry soul whispers,
"Rage and inhumanity
ever will be there, the
gull and rose will not.
So dwell on them before
their time's released."

Day explodes.
Each breath I borrow,
each sight that I acquire,
each harmony I heed, are
gems of dearest worth.

Bellow, calf!
Spread, wild poppies!
Climb, oh bird of light!
Bellow and spread,
climb and thrive!
I rejoice in thee.

By random rains and measured moons,
by toddler cries and old men's sighs,
by all the fears, tears and triumphs
making us so human,
I rejoice my being.

You enter morning,
blessing upon blessings.
For this mystic trek together,
soaring joys and plunging sorrows,
knotted days, unraveled nights,
time we've bled and bred as one,
I rejoice.

I rejoice in thee.

Hymn to Further Days
(On President Obama's Inauguration)

Hear, as hours near.

Hear diverse streams flow to a beckoning ocean.
Hear soaring wings screech freedom.
Listen to twilight's dignity.
Hear with me this pulse of further days.

Sing times when charity's zest melts cold intent,
when self-determined winds chase tyranny's clouds,
when orchards teem with fruits of humbled pride,
and color is an aromatic bloom of brilliant hue.
Such a time is this, a time for humanity.

Beware! Naivety can easily strangle our chorus.
Chance is daughter of Chaos, Certainty son of Folly.
Even hope cannot construe futures forgetful of past.
Let us not forget that September day when carnage consumed.

A 14-year old asked, "Why did it happen?"
I thought to respond, "Because it did."
That is no reply for a 14-year old.
I might have said, "Because a soul exploded."
Instead, I retreated within to tame emotion,
lest fury devour me, to write this:

Freedom's fires are not stoked from without,
but from humanity's needs within.
Should one succeed in dousing our fervor,
liberty's sparks will drift forever,
igniting blazes in other times and places.

That still is no apt reply for a 14-year-old.
For, other fires have other embers.
It is not enough to dampen ill intentions.
We must search within differing souls
to find that common freedom spark
imbued by our God of many mirrors.

Strike this flint of liberty within all.
Stoke flames unloosed of dogma.
Melt long-hardened insecurity, for
intolerance and war are fear's children.

Write no songs of clan or nation,
but of humans and suckling earth.
Tomorrow lies not in vanquishing symbols,
but in nurturing hearts of whatever shape.

All must sing this Hymn to Further Days
for our song to attain its intended harmony.
Only then, may that 14 year-old and other children
laugh and thrive outside uncertainty's shroud.
Only then, may we continue this pilgrims' trek
to whatever we are destined to become.

Sing! Sing until all souls rekindle.
Let earth sing grandeur to the stars,
on this - the most opportune of times.
Sing with me this Hymn to Further Days.

God bless Humanity!

Morning Glory

The heat vent ruffles curtains,
stirs my half-awake, slow-motion mind.
I sit head-to-elbow, elbow-to-chair,
pondering likely prospects of
another dawn thrust upon me.

Will this day provide succor to me,
or must I provide succor to this day?
Will my advancing age entitle me
to a 'get-out-of-day-free' card, or
must I expend dwindling sustenance
to yet another *day-just-a-day*?

If I can postulate long enough,
this knotty issue may resolve itself?

Simplest Truth

The ocean, so plain when pressed
by crowded, dingy clouds.
The ocean, so scintillating, so fresh,
when winds chase drabness away,
allow the sun to etch sea crests.

The dawn, so plain and unmeshed,
when I am sitting alone.
The dawn, so scintillating, so fresh,
when someone appears in the doorway
to share my morning's crest.

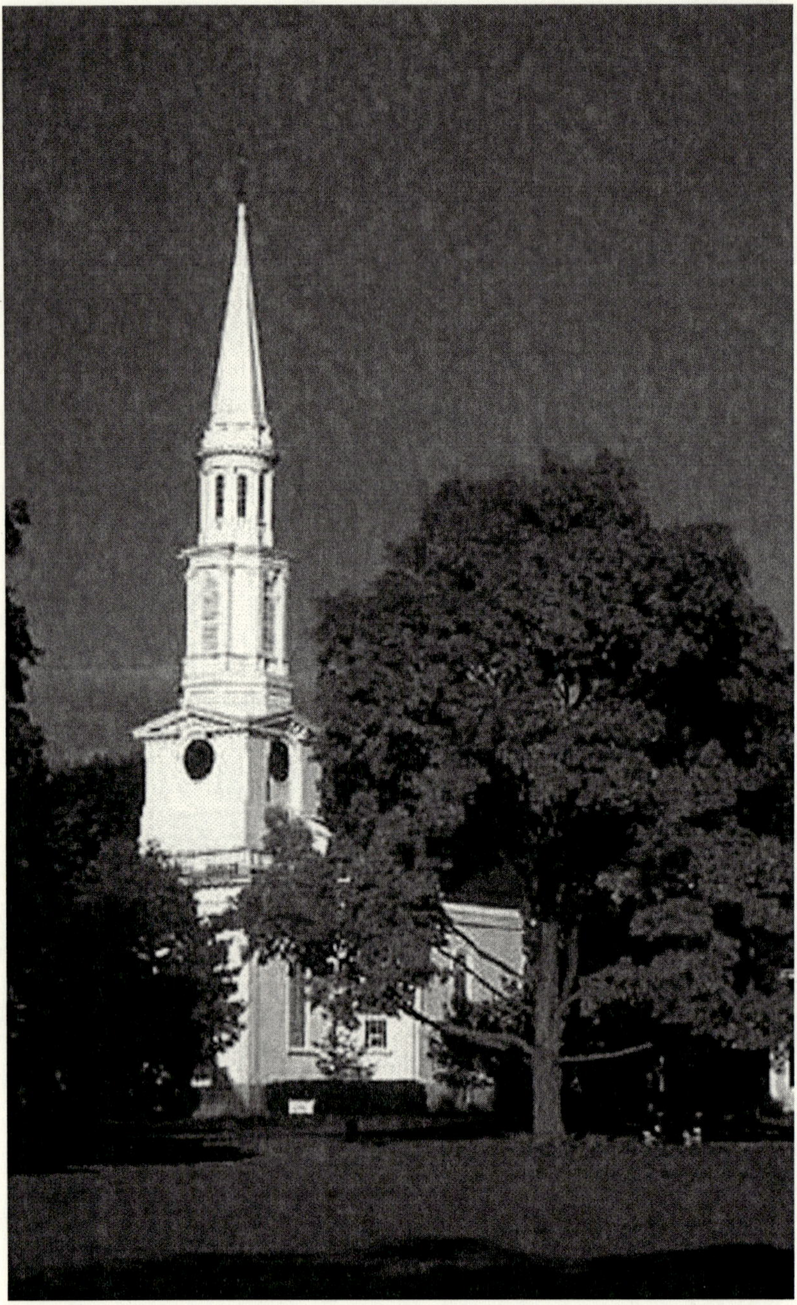

Publication Acknowledgements

Title	Pubication	Date
Inland	SpokeWrite	Spring 2009
Knight of the Sad Countenance	Muse-lings	October 2005
Meaning	*The Haunting* (BookSurge)	2009
Morning Suite	Poetry Now	October 2003
Paean to Being	*The Haunting* (BookSurge)	2009
San Francisco	Muse-lings	October 2005
Whiskey Joe	Poetry Now	May 2005

Dr. Merle Martin

Dr. Merle Martin is author of *The Haunting: Poetic Images of Alaska* and several other books. He is a Professor Emeritus at Sacramento State University and Editor of Remodel Spokane Magazine. Dr. Martin has taught at several universities including ones in Thailand and the Russian Far East. He holds degrees from Texas A&M, Stanford, and the University of California, Berkeley. He was a Lt. Colonel in the Air Force and a former State Director of Logistics for the Alaska Air National Guard. He resides with his wife in Spokane Valley, Washington.

Author photo by: Victoria Shields